essentials

Writing Good Reports

Time-saving books that teach specific skills to busy people, focusing on what really matters; the things that make a difference – the *essentials*. Other books in the series include:

Making Great Presentations

Speaking in Public

Responding to Stress

Succeeding at Interviews

Solving Problems

Hiring People

Getting Started on the Internet

Writing Great Copy

Making the Best Man's Speech

Feeling Good for No Reason

Making the Most of Your Time

For full details please send for a free copy of the latest catalogue. See back cover for address.

The things that really matter about

Writing
Good Reports

John Bowden

MARINO INSTITUTE OF EDUCATION

ESSENTIALS

Published in 1999 by
How To Books Ltd, 3 Newtec Place,
Magdalen Road, Oxford OX4 1RE, United Kingdom
Tel: (01865) 793806   Fax: (01865) 248780
email: info@howtobooks.co.uk
www.howtobooks.co.uk

British Library Cataloguing in Publication Data.
A catalogue record for this book is available from
the British Library.

Edited by David Venner
Cover design by Shireen Nathoo Design
Mind Map® is the registered trade mark of the Buzan Organisation
Produced for How To Books by Deer Park Productions
Typeset by PDQ Typesetting, Newcastle-under-Lyme, Staffordshire
Printed and bound in Great Britain

NOTE: The material contained in this book is set out in good faith for general guidance and no liability can be accepted for loss or expense incurred
as a result of relying in particular circumstances on
statements made in the book. Laws and regulations are complex
and liable to change, and readers should check the current position
with the relevant authorities before making personal arrangements.

ESSENTIALS *is an imprint of*
How To Books

Contents

List of Illustrations

Preface

Writing a report can be described as a career skill. It is not only important as a task that forms part of an increasing number of business jobs; it can also make a huge difference to how you are perceived and even to how you get on in your career. This may not be fair or even reasonable, but it happens. Perception is reality. There is no response other than to consistently produce *excellent* reports.

What you say is important. But how you say it and how it looks are vital in creating a professional report that stands out from the deluge of material your readers inevitably receive. To be successful, a report must be:

- read without undue delay
- understood without undue effort
- accepted and, where appropriate, acted upon.

To achieve these aims you must do more than present relevant facts accurately; you must communicate in a way that is both **acceptable** and **intelligible** to your readers. Writing good reports requires a combination of substance and style: having something worthwhile to say and knowing how to say it effectively.

There are dozens, perhaps hundreds, of different types of report. Yet the **essentials** of effective report writing are the same for all of them, from the most weighty research report to the humblest inter-departmental memo. This book focuses on **the things that should really matter to you**, whatever type of report you may be required to write.

John Bowden

1 Preparing and Planning

To fail to prepare is to prepare to fail.

4

things that
really matter

1 **SETTING YOUR OBJECTIVE**

2 **ASSESSING YOUR READERSHIP**

3 **DECIDING WHAT INFORMATION YOU WILL NEED**

4 **PREPARING YOUR SKELETAL FRAMEWORK**

The importance of preparation and planning cannot be stressed too highly. Often, however, writers simply ignore this aspect or dismiss it as too mechanical to be worthwhile. As a result they plough too quickly into the writing process itself and end up failing to realise their full potential.

Anything you commit to paper before your overall plan has taken shape is likely to be wasted; it will be like a bricklayer starting to build the wall of a house before the architect has drawn up the plans.

The **four things that really matter**, listed above, collectively constitute the planning stage of report writing, and the amount of time and thought you spend on them will make a *vast* difference to the effectiveness of all the work that will follow.

Preparation time is essential. It will be amply repaid when you produce a document which flows smoothly and does not ramble. An hour's structured thinking can save you days of work later.

IS THIS YOU?

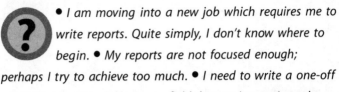

● *I am moving into a new job which requires me to write reports. Quite simply, I don't know where to begin.* ● *My reports are not focused enough; perhaps I try to achieve too much.* ● *I need to write a one-off report. I am a specialist in my field, but an inexperienced communicator.* ● *I have been disappointed in my previous efforts at report writing and want to improve my technique.* ● *I've been producing reports for years. I am quite competent, but feel it's time to add a little polish to my act.*

① SETTING YOUR OBJECTIVE

It is vital to establish your precise objective. You must first be absolutely sure **why** you are going to write. Only then can you even begin to think about **what** you are going to write and **how** you are going to write it.

A clearly defined objective has a number of important benefits:

- It helps you decide what information to include – and leave out.

- It helps you pitch the report at the right level.

- It makes it easier to write the report.

An objective is not what you intend to write, it is what you intend to achieve.

Only by continually thinking about your objective – or **Terms of Reference** – can you expect to remain relevant throughout and ensure that everything that **should** be covered **has** been covered – and that everything that **should not** be covered **has not** been.

Writing a research report is not an objective, it is a **task**.

The **objective** is to extend the readers' knowledge of the world by reducing their uncertainty and increasing their understanding of it. Writing a trouble-shooting report is not an objective, it is a **task**. The **objective** is to locate the cause of some problem and then suggest ways to remove or treat it. Concentrate on the **objective**, not the associated task.

There's one more huge advantage in setting a clear objective. You can go back to the person who asked for the report and ask them to have a look at your objective to make sure they agree with it. If they don't find out **precisely** what they *do* expect from you. By clearing this up at the earliest realistic time, you will have wasted just a few minutes of your time rather than days, weeks or even months.

 ASSESSING YOUR READERSHIP

The next stage is to identify and assess your readership. The detailed content, style and structure of the report can then be matched to the level of knowledge and expertise of this readership. The following questions will prove useful in completing this task:

- Are the readers alike or mixed?
- Are they used to reading and understanding reports?
- How much time will they spend on this report?
- What do they already know?
- What else will they need to know?

These questions are not a complete list but are merely intended to start your thinking regarding the analysis of your **target audience**. It is essential that you have a clear understanding of this group while creating the report so as to focus on *their* needs and expectations.

*A report which is perceived as reader-friendly will always go down
better than one that is introspective.*

 DECIDING WHAT INFORMATION YOU WILL NEED

For some reports, you will need to collect very little
information, while for others you will require a great deal.
You will need to think this through carefully, either on your
own or with other people.

It is often useful to discuss this with the person who
commissioned the report and with prospective readers,
particularly key decision-makers. Are there any specific areas
they would like covered?

*The very fact that people have been consulted at this early stage will
involve them and, psychologically, this will greatly increase the
likelihood of them accepting your conclusions and any
recommendations you subsequently may make.*

You have already written down your overall objective. Take
another look at it and see what it tells you. For example, if
you were asked to investigate the circumstances
surrounding an accident in a canteen kitchen, your
objective could be agreed to be: To investigate how an
employee received injuries from a food mixer whilst working
in the canteen. You can now draw up a **general list** of
areas you will need to cover:

- What happened?
- What were the consequences?
- Was the employee properly trained?
- Was the machine properly maintained?
- Was it avoidable?

*Consider everything, and later check it against your objective to
make sure it's relevant.*

Once you've done this you can start to list **specific** questions that will need to be answered. For example, under 'Was the machine properly maintained?' the supplementary information you will require would include:

- Was a full service record maintained?
- Was the machine in good working order?
- Have any other problems been reported?

You can draw up your lists of **general areas** to be covered and **specific questions** that will need to be asked in any way you like. There are no rules. Use whatever method suits you best. Many writers **mind map**® the information they will need to obtain.

Rather than starting at the top of the page and working down in sentences, lists or words, you begin at the **centre** with your main idea – your objective – and branch out as your information requirements become readily apparent.

Mind mapping® your total research needs has a number of significant advantages over relying on experience, random thoughts or, worst of all, good fortune:

- The objective of the report is more clearly defined.

- All the facts that will be needed are clearly identified.

- Unnecessary facts will not be included.

- The links between the key concepts and facts will immediately be recognisable because of the proximity and connection.

- The nature of the structure allows for easy addition of new thoughts and information.

The open-ended nature of a mind-map will enable the brain to make new connections far more readily. Expect to be surprised.

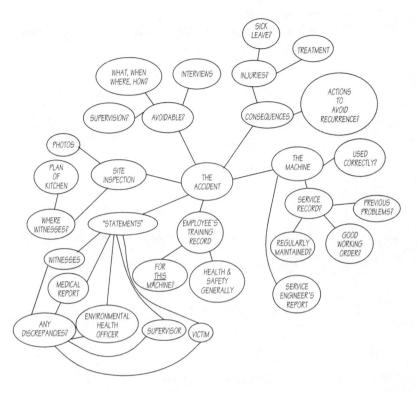

Mind mapping the information you will need.

At this stage what matters is that a **complete picture of information requirements** is seen to emerge. How far does the picture radiate naturally from the central objective? If a thought or fact or idea does not radiate, it will be difficult to make the report coherent and interesting. More importantly, it will not support your objective, so it has no place in the report.

 PREPARING YOUR SKELETAL FRAMEWORK

You are now in a position to think about the overall **plan** of your report. This is known as the **skeletal framework**. It is like drawing up the plans for a new house. Not only will it show your overall **structure**, it will also remind you of the materials (**information**) you will need to gather before the process of construction can begin.

A number of significant benefits will accrue in constructing a skeletal framework. In particular, it will enable you to:

- be sure there is no misunderstanding over the Terms of Reference
- have an overview of the entire report
- be reminded of what information must be collected, what is already available and what is not needed
- order your thoughts before considering how they should be expressed
- appreciate the significance of and the relationship between the various items of information that will be gathered
- identify any gaps in coverage or logic
- maintain a sense of perspective while gathering this information and, later, when writing the report.

A well-planned skeletal framework is the key to effective report writing.

There are three stages involved in the preparation of a skeletal framework:

- Write a **working title**.
- Consider the **overall structure** of the report.
- Decide how information will be presented **within the main body**.

The first step then is to write a **working title**, which defines the subject matter of the document. The title must accurately describe what the text is all about. For the planning phase, use a **functional** title rather than a creative, attention-grabbing title. For example, use 'Why ABC should build a factory in Anytown' rather than 'Anytown: A Town of Growth'.

A functional working title is helpful in continually reminding you of the document's objective.

Save the more creative title for the final, published version of the report, possibly adding the working title as the subtitle.

The second step is to consider the **overall structure**. Reports come in a variety of shapes and sizes and are made up of a variety of sections, or **components**. The choice and combination of components *you* will use should be influenced by the following factors:

- the requirements of the person who commissioned the report
- house style
- custom and convention
- your objective
- your readership
- common sense.

Here is a simple structure that is favoured by many organisations and report writers:

The beginning (or **prelims**)
- Title page
- Contents page
- Summary
- Introduction

The middle

- Main body

The end (or **end matter**)

- Conclusions
- Recommendations (if applicable)
- Appendices

The final step is to consider how information should be presented **within the main body** of the report. If you have already mind mapped® the information you will need to obtain (page 15), you can now reshape your material into a structure that your readers will find both **acceptable** and **intelligible**.

The report on the accident in the canteen would be confusing if it simply recorded the supervisor's, doctor's and engineer's comments in turn. An improvement would be to extract the related parts of their respective evidence and to record them together within appropriate sections or **categories** of the report.

It is better to structure the main body with several short categories, each containing a few subheadings, than to have just a few categories, each with several subheadings, sub-subheadings or even sub-sub-subheadings.

Different levels of category must be organised into a **hierarchy**, with the title at the top of the hierarchy. **Level 1 Categories** are based on **the broad areas that are to be covered**; **Level 2 Categories** relate to the **more detailed findings** which **collectively** cover each of these broad areas. For example:

Working title: Investigation into the accident in the canteen

Main body:

Level 1 Categories: The accident; The consequences; Condition of the machine; Employee training provided.

Level 2 Categories: What it was; Where it occurred; When it occurred; How it occurred (collectively covering 'The accident'); Injuries sustained; Treatment required; Absence from work resulting; Actions taken to avoid recurrence (collectively covering 'The consequences'); and so on.

In addition to the hierarchical organisation, each module or group of categories must be put into a **logical order**. Categories can be considered as one of two types: **verbs** (relating to sequences, actions, events) and **nouns** (relating to people places, ideas).

- **Verb categories** describe **actions**, something that **moves** or **changes** over a **period of time**; they involve **time-sequence information**, such as when each of several events occurred or how the steps of a procedure are performed. This book is structured in this way.

- **Noun categories** tell about something at **a specific point in time**; they include such descriptions as **who, what, why** and **where**.

Verb categories are usually arranged chronologically according to **order of occurrence**; sooner before later (e.g. procedure 1 before procedure 2, cause before effect, stimulus before response, problem before solution, question before answer). For example:

Working title: Introducing Networks
- Using the network
- Setting up your computer to use the network

- Sharing your folders or printers
- Using resources located on other computers
- Connecting to the Internet

Noun categories are sequenced according to **quantity** (e.g. more before less), **quality** (e.g. better before worse), **space** (e.g. high before low), **alphabet** (e.g. A before B), or some other comparative or otherwise logical measure. For example:

Working title: Comparison of Top Three Job Candidates
- Chris Brown
- Kim Jones
- Pat Smith

Once these three stages have been completed, the categories must be suitably numbered. For example:

Results of Investigation into Canteen Accident at ABC Ltd.
1 Summary
2 Introduction
3 The accident
   3.1 What it was
   3.2 Where it occurred
   3.3 When it occurred
   3.4 How it occurred
4 The consequences
   4.1 Injuries sustained
   4.2 Treatment required
   4.3 Absence from working resulting
   4.4 Actions taken to avoid recurrence
5 Condition of the machine
   5.1 Condition at the time of the accident

5.2 Previous service and maintenance record

6　Employee training provided

6.1 General health and safety training

6.2 Specific training relating to the operation of this
machine

7　Conclusions

8　Recommendations

Appendices

1 Plan of kitchen

2 Photographs of kitchen and machine

3 Report of Environmental Health Officer

4 Statement from accident victim

5 Statement from supervisor

6 Statement from Witness A

7 Statement from doctor

8 Statement from service engineer

9 Service record of machine

10 Training record of accident victim

Finally, you should conduct the following six **tests** on **each
module** or **group of categories** within the framework,
starting with the Level 1 Categories and then progressing
module by module to the most detailed level of the
hierarchy:

- **Inclusion test:** Given the heading of the module, are all
appropriate items included? If not, restrict the scope of
the heading to fit the items that are present, or add the
missing items.

- **Exclusion test:** Given the heading of the module, are all
inappropriate items excluded? If not, delete the
inappropriate items, or expand the heading to fit all the

items in the module.

- **Hierarchy test:** Are the items in the module hierarchically parallel? Headings of similar rank should represent topics of roughly equal importance. If they are not, move the problem items to the appropriate level.

- **Sequence test:** Are the items in the appropriate sequence? Determine whether the module is of the verb or noun type, and then decide whether the sequence is most appropriate for each module.

- **Language test:** Are the items in the module grammatically parallel (e.g. all verb types ending in 'ing' or all nouns types ending with the word 'Department')? If not change the wording to achieve consistency.

- **Numbering test:** Is the numbering system appropriate and consistent? Are all Level 1 Categories numbered consistently (3, 4, 5); Level 2 Categories numbered consistently (3.1, 3.2, 4.1, 4.2, 4.3), and so on? Remember that Level 1 Category numbers will need to have been reserved for each component of the report that will be included within the prelims *before* the main body (for example, 1 Summary; 2 Introduction).

These tests collectively provide a comprehensive, yet relatively simple writing tool. You will gain important benefits from consistently applying them:

- they ensure the structural soundness of the text
- they make the subsequent writing process much more straightforward
- they ensure that text will be easier to read and understand.

MAKING WHAT MATTERS WORK FOR YOU

✓ Be crystal clear about your **objective**. Why are you writing this report? What effect do you want it to have on your readers? The status quo is not an option, or there would be no need for the report to be written.

✓ Find out as much about your **audience** as possible. You will say different things, and in different ways, to help achieve your objective when addressing different people.

✓ Think carefully about the **information** you will need. Talk to the person who asked you to write the report and speak to any key readers. What would they like to see included? Don't include anything unless it is relevant and it helps you achieve your objective. Good report writing is often more about what to leave out than what to put in.

✓ Spend as much time as is necessary in designing, testing and revising your **skeletal framework**. It is the **key** to effective report writing. It should not only cover the **structure** and **content** of the report, but also the **relative significance** and **relationship between the main findings**. It has been estimated that 75% of the time spent on effective report writing is devoted to planning. And 75% of that 75% is spent on preparing the optimal framework for **any particular report**.

2 Gathering the Information

Your task now is to locate, collect and handle enough relevant information – the right information – to enable you to put flesh on the bones of your skeletal framework.

5

things that
really matter

1 **LOCATING THE INFORMATION**

2 **OBTAINING THE INFORMATION**

3 **RECORDING YOUR FINDINGS**

4 **EVALUATING AND PRIORITISING YOUR FINDINGS**

5 **COLLATING, SORTING AND GROUPING YOUR FINDINGS**

Once you have carefully planned your report, it is time to carry out all the work that will be necessary before you can actually write it. In other words, you must now undertake your investigation or inquiry.

There are **five steps** that should **always** be taken, albeit briefly, even when writing the most routine of reports. Having a systematic approach to research makes you **treat every report you write seriously**. It forces your thinking to be led by the facts, rather than falling into that dangerous trap of switching to automatic pilot.

It is very important to do the first three – and preferably all five – of the things that really matter **while you are still on site**, not when you get back to your desk. Otherwise you may have to rely on your memory, on someone's uncorroborated evidence over the phone, or – worst of all – trust to luck, before you can complete your report.

IS THIS YOU?

● *I can write well enough, but I've no idea how to undertake a project.* ● *Where on earth can I find current information about that?* ● *My briefcase is full of scribbled notes on scraps of paper. I understand what they mean when I write them, but they're almost meaningless when I read them, sometimes weeks later.* ● *My work involves a good deal of travel. Sometimes I forget to ask some key questions so I have to phone back later. Very embarrassing.* ● *We have a standard report format which means I can't highlight any particularly important findings.*

① LOCATING THE INFORMATION

Now that you have decided what information you will need and constructed a skeletal framework to support it once obtained, it is time to think about the best place to look for each piece of information you require.

There are four possible **sources** of information available to you:

People: you may be able to obtain the information you require from the local, national or international community. Here are just a few possibilities:

- your colleagues
- members of the public
- federations
- pressure groups
- international organisations.

Books and other publications: perhaps the information can be extracted from a printed source, such as:

- reference books

- journals and magazines
- previous reports
- correspondence
- minutes.

Information technology: the information that a computer can put at your fingertips is almost limitless – provided you have an almost limitless budget to pay for software packages, reference CD-Roms and on-line services!

The Internet has already had a significant impact on the scientific, academic and business communities. For example, it has speeded up the process by which ideas are communicated to a large audience. It is often possible to find the latest information in any particular field from one of the Internet's bulletin boards, long before the relevant article or book is published.

Events and places: the information you require may be available at one or more events or places. Here is a small sample of local, national and international possibilities:

- libraries
- museums
- laboratories
- research institutions
- exhibitions.

Be clearly focused. Avoid blind alleys. Keep in mind what essential facts you will need to uncover.

 OBTAINING THE INFORMATION

You can obtain information from any of these sources through **research**. Research consists of a scholarly or scientific investigation or inquiry and can be considered to be either **secondary** or **primary**.

Obtaining information from secondary sources:
secondary sources include information from books, previous reports, computerised databases and the Internet. **Someone else** has already completed an investigation and has **documented** the information. Two of the most common methods of secondary research therefore are:

- reading
- accessing databases.

For a modest monthly budget you can have on-line access to a veritable cornucopia of information, provided you are prepared to put some time and effort into tracking down the facts and figures you really want.

Obtaining information from primary sources: primary sources include **original** data that **you** have obtained and compiled. Two of the most common methods of primary research are:

- surveying
- experimenting.

Surveys are conducted through written **questionnaires, interviews** or **observations**. Experiments test one method against another. In either a survey or an experiment, a **research design** should be developed. A research design includes details such as **sample size, sampling techniques, procedures** and **statistical methods** used.

It is quite possible to write a bad report even after doing good research, but it is impossible to write a good report after doing poor research. The moral is clear: good research is essential.

RECORDING YOUR FINDINGS

Many organisations have their own formal systems for recording information. For example, report writers may be expected to produce **working papers** which may be reviewed before, during and after the production of the report. These papers may also need to be consulted if any statement in that report is challenged, or if some clarification is required. Some organisations will require files of **background information**, or **planning information**, or **progress reports**, or **staff and other resource usage and costs**, or **documents required to generate data**. So *ultimately* you must record your findings in the way that your organisation prescribes.

However, you may have more freedom to choose the methods by which you record your findings *during* the investigation or inquiry. There are many ways of doing this, and each person will favour a particular approach. Two of the best methods of note-taking are:

Traditional notes: here material is condensed using **headings** and **subheadings**, with the most important points being **emphasised**.

When you make traditional notes it is advisable to:

- use loose-leaf paper
- write on one side of the paper only
- double-space your notes
- leave generous margins.

This will allow your notes to be rearranged and added to when required. You must also decide the layout which suits you best, but here are a few guidelines:

- Once you have chosen a layout, stick to it.
- Use a consistent numbering system.

- Use diagrams and illustrations as well as text.
- Use abbreviations, but be clear, simple and consistent.

Patterned notes: this is an alternative type of note-taking which allows you to summarise your understanding and helps you find **links** between **information** and **ideas**.

You start your patterned notes with a central idea in the centre of a page and ideas, concepts and facts spray out from it. This method of note-taking is also known as mind mapping and an example of the technique was provided on page 15.

Do not neglect traditional notes, but seriously consider using patterned notes as well.

 EVALUATING AND PRIORITISING YOUR FINDINGS

Your findings are now recorded in note-form so you will not need to rely on memory. Your next task is to evaluate and prioritise them. You must ask yourself:

- How **reliable** are my findings?
- How **significant** are my findings?

Evaluating reliability: There are four factors by which the reliability of information should be judged: **accuracy**, **objectivity**, **completeness** and **strength.**

- *Accuracy:* Sometimes you can check the data supplied. For example, are the **mathematical calculations** accurate?

If there are too many calculations to check, remember Pareto's principle, which can be paraphrased as: '80% of what is important is represented by 20% of what exists' (so 80% of a company's income will be generated by 20% of its customers). Concentrate on this 20%.

- *Objectivity:* Have **all the major or relevant points of view** been fairly represented? If the subject is controversial, the arguments for both (or all) cases should have been presented. At the very least, the person who provided the information should have made it clear that the views expressed are his or her own, and should then provide references to opposing viewpoints.

Be very wary of statements without supporting evidence.

- *Completeness:* it is often extremely difficult to prove that information is complete or, more accurately, that it is not incomplete. For example, we know of many animals that once inhabited the world. But how can we prove that they were the only ones? How can we prove that unicorns never existed?

What you must ask yourself is whether all relevant information has been provided and whether any attempt has been made to deceive or mislead by omission.

Then look at it from the other side; is all the information provided relevant or is someone trying to 'blind you with science'?

- *Strength:* evidence is **strong** when:
  - It can be verified or re-performed (for example, a scientific experiment).
  - Independent observers have all come to the same conclusion.
  - There have been a large number of consistent observations.
  - It is in agreement with the general body of knowledge.

Conversely, evidence is **weak** when some or all of these conditions cannot be satisfied.

Always differentiate between fact and opinion, and remember that the former provides the far stronger evidence.

Prioritising your findings: how **important** are your findings? What are their **implications**? How **material** are they? Many report writers simply list every piece of information they have gathered without any consideration of its relative importance. This is a mistake because it implies each is of equal weight.

It is important to recognise that there will be a variety of interconnected causes for, and consequences of, an event – and these will not be of equal importance.

What you must do is **highlight** your most significant findings. Once again, you may find it useful to amend your skeletal framework so that your key findings are not 'lost' somewhere within the main body of the report or in an appendix.

But don't overdo it: the more things you highlight, the less powerful each so-called 'highlight' will become.

At the other extreme, ask yourself whether everything you have found is **worth recording** in the report. Perhaps some findings should be placed in an appendix as evidence of work undertaken – or perhaps they should be omitted entirely. If your readers dismiss any of your findings as petty or irrelevant, this can undermine the entire report and severely damage your credibility.

As you prioritise your findings, continually remind yourself that your aim will be to tell your readers everything they need to know, but not to waste their time with trivia.

*Continually ask yourself the 'So what?' question. If you have no
meaningful answer, do not include the fact in the report.*

 COLLATING, SORTING AND GROUPING YOUR FINDINGS
The next stage is to decide where your various findings will
appear in the report and to cross-reference your notes
accordingly. Many word-processing programs contain
features which you may find helpful. However, often a few
dozen good, old-fashioned sheets of cardboard and a pen
are sufficient and effective tools.

There are various ways of collating material. Many report
writers use this method:

- Number all your traditional notes sequentially from page
  1 through to page n (the final page) and/or put numbers
  against every fact, idea or concept which appears on
  your patterned notes.

- Read through them and write down each main point that
  you want to incorporate in the report on a separate
  small sheet of cardboard (paper is more difficult to
  handle and it tends to rip).

- At the same time, write the note number on the card
  and the skeletal framework reference on the notes.

This process doesn't take as long as you might think. You
don't need to write down the details, just the main points
and the cross-references. So amongst your notes you might
have a newspaper cutting – page number 17 of all your
traditional notes – which you have annotated 'See card 6',
and on the corresponding card 6 you may have written,
'The 1999 Take-over Bid, Note 17'.

Once you've been through all your material, you'll
probably have dozens of these cards. Between them, they

hold all the main points and relevant cross-references to your notes that you'll need to write your report.

It is now time to sort and group the cards.

The reason why cards are so useful is that you can easily move them around until you feel they are in their most sensible groups.

At this stage, you may well find it necessary to amend your skeletal framework because some other grouping seems more logical now that you've got the information together. Or perhaps it would be better to split one section of your original framework or merge two together. This is fine – just do whatever seems logical. But whatever revised framework you come up with, before you begin writing and revising, you must confirm that it remains structurally sound by applying those same **six key questions** that appear on pages 21 and 22.

MAKING WHAT MATTERS WORK FOR YOU

✓ Consider carefully where you can obtain each item of information you will need and decide what method(s) of research will be most appropriate – secondary, primary, or both.

✓ It is impossible to write a good report after undertaking poor research. So make sure your research doesn't let you down.

✓ Record your findings in whichever way you find most useful. Later you may also need to transcribe it in the format expected by your organisation.

✓ Decide where your various findings will appear in the report. Ensure important points are highlighted, less important points are recorded within the body of the report and/or in appendices, and unimportant points are omitted. If necessary, revise your skeletal framework.

✓ Before you conclude your investigation or inquiry, be sure that:
   – you have located, obtained and recorded all the information you will   need to write the report
   – you are satisfied that all this information is accurate and reliable.

3 Writing and Revising

*The order of writing and revising is important.
You need to develop a methodical, clinical
approach to the process of ordering, classifying
and sequencing.*

5

**things that
really matter**

1 PRE-WRITING

2 DRAFTING THE MAIN BODY AND APPENDICES

3 DRAFTING THE PRELIMS AND END MATTER

4 CHECKING AND AMENDING THE REPORT

5 ISSUING THE REPORT

If sufficient time and thought have been devoted to
preparing, planning and revising the skeletal framework, you
will now have a practical blueprint for the entire report.
Writing will entail amplifying the points and 'putting flesh
on the bones'.

However, you can't write your introduction until you
know what you're introducing. You can't write your
summary until you know what you're summarising. You can't
make any recommendations until you have reached
meaningful conclusions from a review of your detailed
findings. In other words, you need to write and revise your
report in a **specific, logical order**. In report writing you do
not begin at the beginning, go on till you come to the end
and then stop.

The order of writing and revising is different from the
order of reading. And the correct order of writing, the
correct order of 'putting flesh on the bones' is what this
chapter is all about.

IS THIS YOU?

● *The worst part is getting started. Once I've begun to write I'm OK.* ● *I find that comparatively insignificant issues can dominate my reports and important issues seem to get lost.* ● *I begin with my introduction or preface and later find I have to rewrite it because it doesn't accurately reflect what I go on to say in the main body.* ● *My boss often changes my reports without telling me why.* ● *We write 'team reports'. The problem is they usually end up as a messy patchwork written in a variety of styles.*

PRE-WRITING

Before you begin to draft your report, step back, metaphorically, and take an overview. There should be three aspects to this (five if you are making recommendations), namely:

- **Targeting:** remember your readers. They are the important people. It is all too easy to write for yourself and not for them. No writer can afford to be so self-indulgent.

As a writer, you have to acknowledge your readers' importance and include them. You really have no choice. If you ignore them, they won't be interested in your report. If they're not interested, your report will have failed.

- **Outlining**: remember your objective. Is your general approach appropriate? Think carefully about your overall strategy and the best ways of presenting your arguments to achieve your desired outcome.

In report writing we work backwards from Newton's Law that every action has an equal and opposite reaction. We decide the reaction we want and work back to the words that will produce it.

- **Structuring:** refer to your skeletal framework. Is it wide enough to encompass all the material that must be included to meet your objective – no more and no less? Is it still the optimal structure, or will it need to be revised, perhaps to highlight some particularly important finding?

It is far easier to revise a skeletal framework than to attempt to structure your findings without an initial plan.

- **Developing:** what will you recommend to overcome problems identified?

Your readers may need to know what should be done, by whom, to overcome a specific problem; they will not want to be told that some undefined action should be taken by some unidentified person for no apparent reason.

- **Checking:** are you sure that these recommendations are realistic and practicable?

Do not risk the rejection of a sensible recommendation by asking for too much. The village hall may require greater security, but don't expect it to be protected as thoroughly as Fort Knox.

 DRAFTING THE MAIN BODY AND APPENDICES

Every report will have a main body, be it described as **Findings, Items requiring the attention of the committee, Analysis**, or whatever. This is where your hard evidence must be presented. And some reports will have detailed **Appendices** which support and possibly develop the material provided in the main body. Whatever these components are called in your report, they are the ones that should be written first.

Begin with the section or subsection of the main body, or with the appendix you feel most confident about.

There are two important reasons for doing this:

- For any writer there is little worse than the horror of facing that first blank page. By choosing to write what you find the easiest or most inviting, you avoid this initial trepidation by immediately getting down to writing.

- The more difficult parts of a project seem less forbidding once the easier ones have been accomplished.

Once you have written your detailed findings, try to forget them for a while. Then come back with a fresh mind. Assess what you have **actually written** and **how it comes across**, rather than still thinking about what you had intended to write and get across. Put yourself in your readers' shoes and be highly self-critical. As you read and re-read your draft, you should:

- assess whether the framework is really the most suitable one to present your facts and arguments

- examine the layout and general appearance

- determine whether the tone and balance are correct

- check the accuracy of figures and calculations

- check the use of English, punctuation and spelling.

This self-assessment should give you a good idea of whether it is necessary to restructure your framework and/or rewrite any of the main body or appendices, in order to get your message across as you had intended.

DRAFTING THE PRELIMS AND END MATTER

As we saw in Chapter 1, there is a wide range of other components that could be included within your report. The most common that appear *before* the main body (**prelims**) and *after* it (**end matter**) are the **summary, introduction, conclusions** and **recommendations**.

But in which order should they be drafted? Ask **'CRIS'**: Your **conclusions** must follow logically from your detailed findings. Your **recommendations** must follow logically from your conclusions. Your **introduction** should include everything your readers need to know before they read the rest of the report.

Each of these additional components can now be directly related to what has **actually been written** in the main body and appendices. Another advantage of this approach is that it avoids the danger of writing the report twice: it is very easy for an introduction to develop into a report if the detailed findings have not been written first of all.

While these sections are all important, you must pay particular attention to your **summary**. Make sure that the overall opinion is expressed accurately and unambiguously, and reflects the findings and comments given in the main body and appendices. It must be a true summary of the report and should highlight any areas requiring a particular emphasis. The summary should stimulate the readers' interest by outlining:

- the salient facts
- the main conclusions and recommendations.

A summary must be interesting; if a reader finds it boring, the report will have failed.

CHECKING AND AMENDING THE REPORT

'Hold it two weeks' is a classic rule in advertising. For the report writer this may not be practicable. However, once you have completed your first draft, try to forget about it for a few days – or at least a few hours. Then re-read it. Does it **flow**? Are there adequate **links** and **signposts** for the reader? Can you **justify** everything that you have written? Would you be willing to **say** what you have **written** to the recipients **face-to-face**.? If you would not be willing to say it, do not write it either.

The longer you can leave your review, the more useful and constructive it is likely to be.

After ten minutes you will find yourself attempting to justify and defend every sentence, every word, every comma. After ten days you will find yourself happily revising and even removing entire blocks of text.

Print out a copy of your document. It is far easier to spot mistakes and other shortcomings on hard copy than on screen. Look for any factual or keying errors, or instances of poor presentation. Re-perform the six key tests on your draft that you used to assess your skeletal framework (**Inclusion, Exclusion, Hierarchy, Sequence, Language, Numbering**). Is every section, subsection, paragraph, sentence and word necessary? Are they accurate? Do they convey the meaning you intended?

However, by now you will have read and re-read the draft so often that you may not be able to see the wood for the trees. So ask a sympathetic colleague, who knows about as much about the subject as your readers – but not much more – to give his or her candid comments on the amended report.

It is far easier to detect flaws in other people's writing than in your own.

Are there any obvious errors or ambiguities? What changes or improvements would they suggest? What impact is the report likely to have on your readers? You have been too closely involved to assess this objectively.

It is usual for your line manager to check the draft at this stage. As well as asking the same sorts of question about it as you and your colleague did, your manager will probably be considering wider aspects of the report:

- its technical content
- its overall relevance
- whether it is politically sensitive.

If the report was authorised by a senior officer, your line manager will be particularly concerned that it does credit to the section, firm or profession.

You should *always* be given the opportunity to discuss the reasons for any changes made by your line manager. If this does *not* happen:

- You may feel that this is no more than unjustified criticism.

- You will not learn from the experience as you can only guess what was wrong with your version.

- You may conclude that there is no point in spending so much effort on subsequent reports if they are going to be re-written by superiors.

By now your draft will have so many comments and amendments on it that it almost certainly will need to be reprinted. This may well be the final version of the report. There is no *right* number of rewrites for any given piece of text. Some sections may need several revisions; others require none. One to three rewrites is common. Do as many as necessary to get your report into finished shape.

Rewriting to get it right is an excellent practice; rewriting as a matter of course is a very bad and wasteful practice.

Once the final version is printed, it should be carefully proof-checked. However much time and effort are put into researching and writing the report, the required results will not be achieved without sufficient care being devoted to the process of proofreading. A poorly presented report, full of errors and inconsistencies in layout, has a damaging effect regardless of the quality of content. Mistakes, therefore, must be identified and corrected; there really is no excuse for failing to this properly.

Proofreading your own work is difficult and inefficient. Because you are so familiar with the report, you tend to race through and think of the bigger picture – the next report. Someone else who has not been working on the report can give it a much fresher and more objective scrutiny.

Here are some useful proofreading techniques:

- Print out a copy of the report. Spell-checkers and grammar-checkers miss things, and people do not read on screen with the same diligence as they read from the printed page.

- Use a ruler to slow down your reading and make yourself read line by line.

- Read the report out aloud. This process slows down your reading and makes you listen to how it sounds.

- Limit your proofreading to one small section at a time. Then take a small break before proceeding to the next small section.

- Try to proofread when you know you will have peace and quiet and can avoid interruptions from telephones or visitors.

 ISSUING THE REPORT

In some organisations the report would now be issued. In others, the following final steps are taken:

- **Discussion:** the writer discusses his or her findings with the key recipients and confirms the accuracy of significant facts.

- **Clearing:** any corrective action is agreed and/or the report is amended in the light of any mistakes or misapprehensions shown to have occurred during the investigation.

- **Circulation:** the revised report, clearly annotated 'Draft' on the cover and on every page, is circulated.

- **Agreeing:** the findings are agreed.

- **Issuing:** the final report is issued.

There are important advantages in following the above additional steps:

- It paves the way for the recommendations.

- It prepares the recipients for any criticisms which may be in the final report.

- It enables the writer to adapt the tone and emphasis of the report in light of the recipients' initial reactions.

- It increases the probability that the findings will be accepted if they have been fully discussed and the recipients' views have been taken into account.

- It enables the writer to avoid errors and

misunderstandings which would otherwise undermine his or her credibility and damage the department's or company's reputation.

The responsibility for final approval of the report often rests with the writer's line manager. Once this approval has been obtained, arrange for or make the correct number of bound copies, retaining at least one of them.

By publication day, the names, addresses and designations of all the recipients should be known and checked. Envelopes, wrappers and labels should have been made up, and covering letters or compliment slips prepared to explain why the report has been sent and to provide a contact point (probably you) if further enquiry or comment is desired.

Record full details of all issues in a register and try to ensure that each person receives their copy at the same time.

MAKING WHAT MATTERS WORK FOR YOU

✓ Before you begin to draft your report, take an overview. Are you tackling the subject in the best way to achieve your objective with this readership? Will you need to revise your skeletal framework, perhaps to highlight some important finding?

✓ Draft your main body and any appendices first.

✓ Then go on to write your conclusions, any recommendations, introduction and summary.

✓ Check the content and presentation of your report very carefully. Ask a sympathetic colleague to take a look as well before passing the revised document to your line manager.

✓ Ensure that all necessary arrangements have been made before issuing the report.

4 Adopting an Appropriate Style

Successful report writing requires a combination of substance and style: having something worthwhile to say and knowing how to say it effectively.

3
things that
really matter

1 MAKING IT READABLE

2 ACHIEVING A GOOD STYLE

3 COMMUNICATING MORE EFFECTIVELY

The word 'style' is not used here – as it is normally used in discussing literature – as a term for appraising the quality of a writer's method of expression. A person may be well-educated and write in an excellent literary style, yet use bad style in writing a report – because he or she fails to **communicate** with readers. You must do more than **present** relevant facts accurately; you must **convey** them in a way that is both **acceptable** and **intelligible** to your readers.

Good style in report writing means getting your message across accurately and quickly to the reader each time you write. Every situation on which a report is prepared will vary, at least slightly. If this were not so, there would be no need for the report to be written. The expression of every point must therefore be drafted with the new situation in mind. Orthodoxy and imitation (for their own sake) are the refuge of the poor report writer.

IS THIS YOU?

● I find it difficult to write readable reports because of the highly technical nature of the content. ● My style has been criticised as poor but nobody will say what specific improvements they expect. ● I find it difficult to pitch my reports at the right level. ● Some people say my reports are too formal while others say the same reports are spot on. It's very odd. ● Sometimes I can get a lot of writing done in an hour or so; other times I seem to have got nowhere after a whole day.

MAKING IT READABLE

Research into what makes a piece of writing **readable** started in America about seventy years ago. Experts nowadays agree that the factors that most affect readability are:

- an attractive appearance
- non-technical subject matter
- a clear and direct style
- short sentences
- short and familiar words.

Several software **grammar-checkers** aspire to provide general advice on readability. While each has at least something to offer, they disregard such things as:

- the way the information is organised
- how it looks on the page
- the readers' motivation and level of prior knowledge.

They give only the merest hint about how to write better text and they encourage the idea that a clear document is one that scores well on a formula. **Few serious writers bother with them.**

Keeping the average length of sentences short is one of the simplest and best ways of ensuring readability.

Aim for an average sentence length of less than twenty words. This does not mean, of course, that every sentence in a section must contain no more than twenty words. In fact, it is preferable to vary the lengths and constructions of sentences, otherwise your writing will have a staccato rhythm or a terseness which many readers may find either childish or otherwise irritating. (That sentence has thirty-four words.)

 ACHIEVING A GOOD STYLE

There are numerous ways in which you can bring an individuality to whatever you write which will not only enable you to communicate more effectively with other people, but also give your writing extra colour and impact at the same time. Here are some guidelines:

'Think audience': you have already identified and assessed your readers. If you want their approval for your report, adapt your writing style to *their* idea of what constitutes good English, *not yours*. Readers are diverse. For example, they may be:

- people with a more traditional style of English than yours
- people with a more modern style of English than yours
- people for whom English is not their first language.

Some other factors that will affect your choice of style are:

- *Age*: the young prefer a different approach from the elderly.

- *Background, education and experience*: your readers may be professional people, technical experts, work colleagues. On the other hand, they may be ordinary lay people with a general interest in the subject.

- *Outlook and attitudes*: look for shared values, personal preferences, differences in social class and culture.

There is only one ultimate judge of the effectiveness of a report – and that is its readers. Readers are supreme.

Get the tone right: you must express yourself in a way that invokes the **right feelings** in your readers. Tone is an important element of the way you communicate your attitudes about the subject to the intended readership. Make sure you:

- avoid inappropriate use of humour, levity, frivolity, satire, sarcasm and irony

- avoid writing in a style which is too formal, flowery, stiff or stilted

- avoid a pompous or patronising manner.

You would say **different things** and discuss them in **different ways** when speaking to a boss, a colleague, a subordinate, a customer, a member of the public. It should be the same when you write a report. In other words, you must get the **tone** right for this particular readership.

Reports are important documents. They should be written in a style that is serious without ever becoming solemn.

Be unobtrusive: if readers become aware of the style it probably means that the writing is pretentious, or ostentatious, or ambiguous, or difficult to read. Above all else, the writing should be easy to read. Good style is good manners.

Be objective: a report should not be an essay reflecting personal emotions and opinions. You must look at all sides of a problem with an **open mind** before stating your conclusions. The role is similar to that of a sports referee or a High Court judge. In these situations, decisions are based on the results, the evidence, or an interpretation of the evidence – not on personal opinions and feelings.

Making it clear that you have an **open mind** when writing your report will, in most cases, make your conclusions and recommendations more acceptable to your readers. If a personal bias is detected, the reader may become suspicious of the accuracy of the report. The emphasis, therefore, should be on the **factual material** presented and the **conclusion drawn** rather than on any personal beliefs, biases or prejudices.

Be concise: *veni, vidi, vici* (I came, I saw, I conquered). That is how Julius Caesar reported his visit to our shores. While none of your reports will be as short as this, you should aim to keep them concise. In doing this, do not mistake brevity for conciseness. A report may be brief because it omits important information. A concise report, on the other hand, is **short** but still contains all the **essential details**.

To ensure you do not include material which can safely be left out, you should not ask, 'Can this information be included?' Rather, you should ask: 'It is *necessary* for this information to be included?' In this way, you will be sure to put in your report only as much information as your readers need in order to respond as you wish them to.

Keep it simple: many problems in communicating are caused by making things more difficult than they need be. The problem of how to keep things simple is particularly acute for technical writers. It is all too easy for them to shrug their shoulders and tell themselves that it is not their fault that the information is complex and their readers will just have to follow as best they can. This is simply not good enough.

The rewards of writing simply are considerable. Readers will at least understand what has been said and will be more likely to respond favourably to conclusions drawn and recommendations made. They will form a higher opinion of the writer and they will read subsequent reports with greater attention and enthusiasm. These are achievements not to be undervalued.

 COMMUNICATING MORE EFFECTIVELY

Top sportspeople are never satisfied with their game. They know that only by continually analysing their technique and making any necessary changes can they hope to remain successful sportspeople. It is the same with people who want to become, and then remain, successful report writers.

There are several well-known and well-tested pieces of advice to people who want to communicate more effectively on paper. Here are some that should prove particularly valuable to report writers.

Thinking about your content

Always begin by saying what you have been asked to do, who asked you and when. Say how, where and when you have done it, and with whose help. Always explain what you are talking about.

Never overestimate your readers' knowledge; never underestimate their intelligence.

- You cannot explain the present without first explaining

the past. Begin at the beginning. How have things come to where they are now?

- Differentiate between the main facts and the details and examples which illustrate them.

- Try to consolidate highly factual references into self-contained sections which will be seen as help for those who require it, but not as required reading for those who do not.

- Always make it clear what you have accepted, and what you have verified. When you have verified something, say how.

- Avoid producing too many figures and too few explanations. Restrict figures to those which are meaningful and make sure they are consistently produced and interpreted.

- Never assume that readers will draw the right conclusion from figures. They may quite easily not be reading them at all when they read the text; or they may read them and draw the wrong conclusion; or they may fail to draw any conclusion. Always say in words what they tell readers.

- Be specific. Words like 'mostly', 'largely' and 'substantially' merely raise the question 'how much?'. Say instead 'three-quarters', 'two-thirds', 'about half'; there is no need to be finicky, but you must say what you mean.

Drafting the report

- Reserve a quiet room where you can write your report with minimal distractions.

- Try to write your report over consecutive days.

You will find that in two days you will achieve three times what you would in one; in four days you will do four times what you might in two.

- Write in bursts of about forty minutes to an hour, each followed by a short break.

- Never start a writing session without being clear what you intend to achieve.

- Be flexible. You may have to postpone a writing session to do some other work. However, flexibility works both ways, so make the most of any unexpected writing opportunities.

- Remember that a ten-minute break can often be more useful than a hour sitting at your desk.

- Once you have started, keep the momentum going. Do not be overconcerned with writing conventions at this stage. There will be time for this later.

- Read a passage aloud to yourself. If it sounds like the latest news from Kosovo, or staccato or complicated, you are failing.

- Allow a period of twenty-four hours to elapse between your first draft and its revision. If you can leave it longer, so much the better. If you are really under pressure and it simply is not possible to leave it overnight, at least try to leave it over a lunch or coffee break.

It is important that you should have a period of time, however short, when you can think of other things. In this way, when you come back to your report, you can look at it with a degree of objectivity.

MARINO INSTITUTE OF EDUCATION

MAKING WHAT MATTERS WORK FOR YOU

✓ Make sure your report is readable. Give it an attractive appearance; a clear and direct style; and, whenever possible, non-technical subject matter described in short and familiar words in short sentences.

✓ Write for your readers, not yourself. Make things as easy as possible for them.

✓ Never be totally satisfied with your writing. Continually strive for improvements. Think not only about **what** you should write and **how** you should write it, but also **when** you should write and **where** you should write it.

5 Using Good English

*Your report will be regarded as flawed and
viewed with scepticism if it contains errors in the
proper use of English – even if the report has a
wealth of technical, scientific or creative
information.*

5

things that
really matter

1 **UNDERSTANDING BASIC GRAMMAR**

2 **UNDERSTANDING SYNTAX**

3 **USING PUNCTUATION CORRECTLY**

4 **CHOOSING YOUR WORDS CAREFULLY**

5 **SPELLING CORRECTLY**

Any reader whose use of English is good is likely to judge
you on *your* use of English. So it's in your interest to brush
up on any problem areas you have. It can make a big
difference to the impact of your reports. For your own sake,
if you're not sure of something, don't guess – look it up.

In report writing, accuracy and precision are essential.
Your writing must be concise, unambiguous and
authoritative – and yet be attractive to read. If it is not, this
will reflect badly upon you. At best your reports will be
vague and misleading; at worst they will be confusing and
inaccurate. Poor grammar, sloppy syntax, misspelled words
and other infelicities impede communication and advance
only misunderstanding and confusion.

You do not need to have a detailed knowledge of the
correct use of English, but you do need to know the basic
rules and the remedies for the most common problems
report writers encounter. So here, in a nutshell, are those
rules and remedies.

IS THIS YOU?

• *I wasn't taught grammar at school.* • *My spelling is atrocious!* • *My punctuation consists of full stops and the occasional comma.* • *I try to impress my readers with long, complex words, but I'm not sure it's working!* • *Syntax? Are they even taxing that now?*

① UNDERSTANDING BASIC GRAMMAR

Grammar is the science of structure and usages of language. It provides a system of general principles for writing good English. This section is *not* intended to be a grammar lesson. It simply deals with the **essentials of grammar** that every report writer needs to know.

You need to be aware of the main 'parts of speech'. After all, how you can 'cut down on your use of adjectives', or whatever else you may be asked to do by a 'traditionalist', if you do not even know what adjectives are?

So here are some important definitions:

- **Paragraphs** are groups of sentences which are linked together in a logical manner and share a common theme.

- **Sentences** are groups of words which must include a noun (or pronoun) and a verb.

- **Nouns** are naming words and can be either concrete or abstract. A **concrete noun** may be a person, place or thing (*Fred, London, table*). **Abstract nouns** may express qualities, feelings and ideas (*greenness, happiness, truth*).

- **Pronouns** are words that can replace nouns in a sentence (*I, her, they*).

- **Verbs** are doing words (*danced, ate, wrote*).

- **Adverbs** are used to extend the meaning of a verb (*quickly, quietly, jokingly*).

- **Adjectives** provide further information about nouns (*big, purple, ugly*).

- **Prepositions** are words used immediately before a noun or pronoun, to show how it relates to another person or object referred to in the sentence (*with, by, for*).

- **Conjunctions** are linking words used to join ideas together by acting as a bridge between words, phrases or sentences (*and, but, or*).

 UNDERSTANDING SYNTAX

Syntax deals with the relations of words or groups of words to one another in sentences.

That is what good writing is all about: the right words in the right order. The more precise this order, the more certain that what is written will not be misunderstood. In report writing, precision and accuracy are essential.

Writers often look at their work and have an uneasy feeling that it is not quite right, but do not know why. Understanding the basic rules of syntax helps identify the malady and its root cause. The cure then presents itself. Volumes have been written on syntax. An understanding of the key rules and examples of their violation will significantly improve your writing.

Avoid the careless positioning of words: this can cause misunderstanding and confusion.

not The headmaster was urged to take a strong line on absenteeism by the board of governors.

but The headmaster was urged by the board of governors to take a strong line on absenteeism.

Remember the subject: illogical statements often result from forgetting the subject of the sentence.

not The policy provides as a maximum reserve 25% of the annual dwelling rent schedule and is accumulated at the rate of 10%.
(The subject is 'policy'. This sentence says that the policy is accumulated at the rate of 10%.)

but The policy provides as a maximum reserve 25% of the annual dwelling rent schedule. The reserve is accumulated at the rate of 10%.

Prefer the positive: try to use positive statements wherever possible.

not We do not believe the backup files are adequate.

but We believe the backup files are inadequate.

Place emphasis at the end: the end of the sentence is where the strength is. The end remains freshest in the reader's mind.

not With a little clarification, the subcontractor would have solved the difficulties occasioned by the specification changes more readily.

but With a little clarification, the subcontractor would have solved more readily the difficulties occasioned by the specification changes.

USING PUNCTUATION CORRECTLY

The purpose of punctuation is simply to make it easier for the reader to understand the text.

A good way to check your punctuation is to read aloud. Whenever you pause or change the inflexion in your choice, you should use some form of punctuation mark.

But which? The answer obviously is important. If you use the wrong one, or put it in the wrong place, you can give a sentence a meaning which you did not intend. Consider the following eight words when punctuated in different ways:

The man said the woman was a fool.

The man said, 'The woman was a fool.'

'The man,' said the woman, 'was a fool.'

The first statement gives the **reported** speech of the **man**; the second gives the **actual** speech of the **man**; the third gives the **actual** speech of the **woman**.

Here are a few guidelines concerning the most common types of punctuation:

- Use a full stop to end a sentence. (*Jesus wept.*)

- Use a full stop after abbreviations. (*km., Nat. Hist.*)

- Use a comma to separate words, phrases and clauses in a series. (*We considered glass, plastic, polythene and polystyrene.*)

- Use a comma between two adjectives. (*A big, red book.*)

- Use a colon before a list of items or a series of words. (*The following people are exempt: Tom, Dick and Harry.*)

- Use a colon to introduce an explanatory statement. (*This is our decision: to accept the offer and sell the factory.*)

- Use a semi-colon to separate phrases in which a comma already exists. (*The men worked in the fields; the women, in the factory; the children, in the school.*)

- Use a semi-colon to join independent clauses not separated by a conjunction such as *and, but* or *or*. (*The investigation is completed; the report will be issued next week.*)

- Use quotation marks to enclose a direct quotation. (*As Wellington said, 'publish and be damned.'*)

- Use quotation marks to enclose titles, words or phrases borrowed from others or used in a special way. (*A 'magic' atmosphere was created.*)

- The apostrophe shows possession. Use before the final s if singular, use after the s if plural. (*Mark's report; the girls' horse.*)

- Use an apostrophe to shorten a word. Place it above the space created by the removal of the letter. (*isn't; don't.*)

- Use parenthesis to enclose explanatory words. (*Report writers must be aware of the main principles of the law of libel [defamation published in a permanent form].*)

- Use a question mark to end a sentence containing a query. (*That is quite straightforward, isn't it?*)

- Use an exclamation mark to suggest a sudden change of emotion. (*Use them sparingly!*)

④ CHOOSING YOUR WORDS CAREFULLY

When children are taught English at school, they are encouraged to use longer and longer words in ever more complex sentences. Paradoxically, the report writer should be encouraged to do just the opposite. Generally, prefer short words in short sentences: the right word, however modest, is never undignified.

Prefer plain English: write to express, not to impress. Carefully used, plain English will reveal your competence far better than the flowery or wooden style of so many report writers.

not The ready availability of computer-based tutorials associated with applications software has become prevalent since the development of Microsoft Windows.

but Computer-based tutorials associated with applications software have become readily available since the development of Microsoft Windows.

Use words that act: use live, active verbs. Verbs converted into nouns are difficult to read. Nouns should be **visual**: purchase orders, computer, widgets. Verbs turned into nouns are not visual and are hard to grasp: subsidisation, reconciliation, containment.

not The elimination of field bonuses could be accomplished.

but Field bonuses could be eliminated.

Avoid overwriting and padding: some words and phrases keep cropping up in reports, yet they add nothing to the message and can often be removed without changing the meaning or the tone. Try leaving them out of your writing. You will find your sentences survive, succeed and even flourish without them.

not During the course of our review, it was established that Accounts Receivable follows up delinquent accounts only.

but Accounts Receivable follows up delinquent accounts only.

Avoid sexist language: the tone of your writing should not reflect a gender bias – or any other type of bias, such as race, religion, age or disability.

not A good report writer knows he must be politically correct.

but Good report writers know they must be politically correct.

However, it is not easy to prepare a long report which is entirely gender-neutral. To do so tends to produce immoderately long sentences, excessive use of the passive and, sometimes, ambiguous writing. In addition, it seems reasonable that where there is an overwhelming majority of one sex in the report's readership, the use of pronouns should reflect this.

⑤ SPELLING CORRECTLY

To many people, incorrect spelling indicates carelessness and lack of attention to detail. This impression must be avoided. You should therefore have a good dictionary and always refer to it if you are unsure about a word's spelling, or about its precise meaning or usage. No computer spell-checker will ever identify every misused or confused word. You have to establish the **correct spelling** from the **context**.

Here are some rules and guidelines which will help you avoid many problematic areas.

- Be careful not to omit part of a word (*accidentally*, not *accidently*).

- Do not join up two separate words (*in fact* not *infact*).

- 'i' before 'e', except after 'c' (*field, yield, receive*). But beware of some *weird* exceptions (*neither, either, leisure*).

- The prefix 'dis' is not hyphenated (*discontinue* not *dis-continue*).

- The prefix 'sub' is not normally hyphenated (*subeditor* not *sub-editor*).

- The prefix 'un' is not normally hyphenated (*uncertified* not *un-certified*).

- To form the plural of words ending in 'y': if there is a consonant immediately before the 'y' in the singular, then the plural is 'ies' (*lady – ladies*). If there is a vowel immediately before the 'y' in the singular, then the plural is 'ys' (*valley – valleys*).

- To form the plurals of words ending in 'ch', 'x', 'sh' or 'ss': add 'es' (*church – churches, box – boxes, dish – dishes, mass – masses*).

Finally, and by way of a little light relief, here are twenty statements, each of which is itself a demonstration of the fault it describes:

- First and foremost, avoid clichés like the plague.

- A verb have to agree with its subject.

- There is no excuse for incorect spelling.

- Avoid abstract nouns, in truth they are not readily understood.

- Never use no double negatives.

- It makes sense not to use the same word in two senses in the same sentence.

- It is pathetic and criminal to use emotive language.

- If you re-read your work, you will find on re-reading it that a great deal of repetition can be avoided by re-reading and editing.

- 'Avoid overuse of "quotation marks" '.

- Avoid all un-necessary hyphens.

- Use commas only, when necessary.

- Do not overuse exclamation marks!!!

- Don't use contractions in formal writing.

- Always avoid all awkward and affected alliteration.

- Avoid using the same word over and over and over again.

- Verily it is incumbent upon you to avoid ensamples of archaic words.

- Avoid mixed metaphors; with enough time on your hands you should never end up with egg on your face.

- Everyone should be careful to use a singular pronoun with singular nouns in their writing.

- Make sure you never a word out.

- *Le mot de la fin*: do not use foreign words or phrases if there are good English equivalent words or phrases.

MAKING WHAT MATTERS WORK FOR YOU

✓ The **correct use of English** almost certainly **matters** to at least some of your readers. For that reason alone, it has to matter to you.

✓ Whenever possible, prefer **short words** in short sentences: the right word, however modest, is never undignified.

✓ If you are unsure about any point of English usage, don't guess – **look it up**.

✓ Get yourself a good, up-to-date **dictionary**. Words get added every new edition, others disappear, and yet others change their meanings. But you cannot find a word you have forgotten or do not know in a dictionary. Look up a word of similar meaning in a **thesaurus** and you will find a variety of words and expressions which should include the one in the back of your mind, or perhaps an unfamiliar word which, when checked in a dictionary, proves even more appropriate.

✓ If you write reports regularly, invest in one or more of these specialist books: *The Complete Plain Words* by Sir Ernest Gowers, *Fowler's Modern English Usage* edited by Dr Robert Burchfield, *English Our English* by Keith Waterhouse.

6 Adding the Final Touches

A report needs to be eye-catching and appealing to readers. While the contents are important, other less obvious factors can make or break a report.

3

things that
really matter

1 **WORD PROCESSING AND DESKTOP PUBLISHING**

2 **REFINING LAYOUT AND DESIGN**

3 **USING ILLUSTRATIONS**

Technology provides new, exciting and better ways of improving the presentation of a report. A computer equipped with word processing or desktop publishing software not only makes the work easier but also provides the opportunity for you to create a report every bit as polished and professional as one produced by an expert team including a writer, typist, typesetter and graphic artist.

What you say is important. But how you say it and **how it looks** are vital in creating a high-impact report that stands out from the deluge of material your audience inevitably receives. This will give you that all-important competitive edge in grabbing attention, making your case and selling your ideas.

No longer do your reports have to look like diaries or essays. Instead they can look like professional publications. From this chapter, you will learn the things that really matter if you transform your tired old reports into attractive, compelling documents with that certain winning look.

IS THIS YOU?

● *I want to write reports for the twenty-first century;
but they look like they were produced in the
nineteenth!* ● *I try to keep my reports short by
cramming in as much as possible onto each page.* ● *My
reports look like school essays.* ● *I don't know what kind of
illustrations to include.* ● *Today's technology frightens me;
give me a quill every time!*

WORD PROCESSING AND DESKTOP PUBLISHING

Unless you are using a steam-driven PC, you will have a
Windows environment which allows you to work **wysiwyg**.
Pronounced **whizzywig**, this acronym stands for **what you
see is what you get**. In other words, what you see on
screen is an accurate representation of how the document
you are working on will print out.

*You can fine-tune the appearance of your report until you are
completely happy with the result.*

Flexibility is the key attribute of word processing and
desktop publishing. Once you have got your text on screen,
you can edit it, format it, save your work as a file and print
it out. Whole blocks of text can be inserted or deleted in
the middle of a report with everything else moving around
to accommodate the change. Paragraphs can be shifted
from one section of a report to another. Sentences can be
amended. Words can be highlighted. In short, **you can do
pretty much what you like with it.**

As well as providing **basic tools** for drawing lines, boxes
and other basic graphic embellishments, most word
processors allow graphics and tabular information to be
imported from other programs – including accounts
packages and spreadsheets that can prepare charts and
tables from the data they hold.

If you have **standard reports** that need to be revised each time they are used, you can create them as **templates**, then **personalise** copies just before they are printed without the need to retype from scratch or take the unprofessional-looking route of typing or writing onto a photocopied standard report. Facilities for **numbering pages**, providing **headers and footers** and compiling a **basic index** should be found in most word processors, which can take another level of tedious work out of producing reports.

On the **design** front, you can expect **style** functions that allow you to save the attributes of text – **font, size, colour** and so on – as a style you can apply easily to sections of text you highlight using the mouse. This facility helps to keep **consistency** both within a report and between reports. You can change the fonts that you use in a report pretty much at will – providing you have installed fonts under the Windows operating system.

Reports of today do not have to look like reports.

You may wish to consider obtaining **add-on packages** in order to improve the more popular word-processing packages. **Task-specific programs** that help you structure, say, a marketing plan can help you enter new fields by providing the examples and expertise needed to create detailed and competent specialist reports.

There are numerous **business-specific applications** that are designed to address particular sectors of commerce or industry. These are referred to as **'vertical' applications**. Some can be applied generally, such as computer-aided design (CAD) packages, but many are only relevant to one field – estate agency, insurance or the like.

Modern word processors and desktop publishing packages present opportunities to the report writer that were unthinkable only a few years ago.

Here are five points to bear in mind when using a word processor to create polished and readable reports:

- Unless you are a graphic designer or have a real need to produce documents for professional printing, you are unlikely to need highly sophisticated software.

- Don't use so many special effects that they cease to be special. Your purpose is to communicate **simply** and **effectively** with your readers.

- Keep **paragraphs** fairly **short** (five to eight lines, on average) – particularly when using two- or three-column layouts.

- Consider setting up a **'house style'** to use in your reports, keeping the number of fonts to a minimum but using standard, attractive layouts. A set of templates can then be used as the starting point for all your documents.

- Develop a **filing system** on your computer so you can easily find and reload reports. If you are dealing with a large number of reports, check that your word processor can search by summary information or the content of a report, rather than just the filename under which reports have been saved.

 REFINING LAYOUT AND DESIGN

Many considerations and decisions are required when choosing your overall layout and design. In particular, you will need to think about:

Format: the format of your report is important in ensuring that it will receive favourable notice and attention. All reports should be attractively produced in an easy-to-read layout, but the need may be even greater if the object is to recommend or persuade.

The value of good design is that it gains the attention of readers and makes the task of reading easier. Formats for a report include:

- *Traditional manuscript*: used for traditional, formal reports. The finished product today can be a professional-looking document, rather than yesterday's style.

- *Memo* and *letter*: used respectively to communicate with people inside and outside the company.

- *Form*: used when it is necessary to provide information regularly and in a consistent format.

- *Newsletter*: used to communicate information to a special interest group.

- *Brochure*: used in almost every area of business; for example, for advertising a product or an event.

Margins and spacing: it is far easier for a reader to assimilate information presented in small sections than in huge, uninterrupted blocks of print. Pages with too much type and artwork give the appearance of being too heavy and hard to read.

Double-space your text and provide fairly wide margins. Leave at least 50% of **white space** on each page. Break up text by using the technique of listing by means of bullet, checkmark or arrow. This will not only help the reader, but also give your report a professional look.

Headings and subheadings: these help busy readers of today by identifying and labelling blocks of type. They are not standard. You must invent them. Make sure that they:

- cover all the ground (collectively)

- do not overlap (although the same information may appear under more than one heading if it supports more than one argument)

- are never vague (for example, avoid headings such as 'General', 'Miscellaneous' and 'Other').

Once you have introduced a topic with a heading or subheading, you cannot leave that topic and move on to another until you provide another heading or subheading. For this reason subheadings should not repeat information provided in headings. For example, if your heading is 'ABC Limited', your subheadings could be 'Production Department', 'Accounts Department' and 'Personnel Department'. There is no need to write, 'ABC Limited – Production Department'.

The title of the report should be more prominent in Level 1 Category headings, which, in turn, should be more prominent than Category 2 headings – and so on. Similarly, headings of the same rank should represent topics of roughly equal importance. There is a paradox here:

The more prominent the heading, the less detailed and specific the text below it; the less prominent the heading, the more specific and detailed the text below it.

Numbering: the role of numbering systems is simply to identify the various components of a report for reference and indexing purposes. There are two aspects to this:

- numbering pages
- numbering sections and paragraphs.

Pages: any time you have more than one or two pages, you need to number them. Computer software has the capability of performing this function automatically, but you must determine where you want the page numbers. Several choices are acceptable – the upper or lower outside corners or the middle of the bottom of the page. Placing numbers on the outside corners allows readers to locate a specific page more easily when scanning through a report.

Sections and paragraphs: for many writers the numbering seems to determine the structure of the report, rather than the other way round. Keep your method as simple as possible. The most popular scheme of numbering is the all-decimal system (1, 1.1, 1.2, 1.3, 2, 2.1, 2.2, 2.3). Reports numbered this way are clear and unambiguous.

 USING ILLUSTRATIONS

Well-produced and **appropriate** illustrations really enhance a report. They make the information readily understandable, easily digestible and memorable. It is much easier to assimilate information presented pictorially. Anything on a page other than text is either artwork or graphics. The word **artwork** refers to the **images** in the report, such as photographs, drawings and cartoons; **graphics** are the **image enhancements**, such as lines, boxes and background tints.

When should you use illustrations?

Illustrations are useful only when they are easier to understand than the words or figures they represent.

Artwork and graphics should clarify, add to, illustrate or enhance the document in some way. They should not be used without a specific reason or purpose. Otherwise, they will merely distract and confuse your readers.

Ask yourself the 'So what?' question: does every illustration have something to say within the overall context of the report? If there is no meaningful answer to 'So what?', then the illustration is worthless. If you have a positive answer to the question, then the illustration *should* be included.

Where should you place the illustrations? Is the illustration **fundamental** to the arguments in the text, or **supplementary** to them? If the reader **needs** to see an illustration in order to understand the text – or if it is referred to several times – it should be placed within the main body of the report. If the reader does not need to see it, it may be preferable to place it in an appendix, particularly if there are several other illustrations.

Ask yourself whether the illustration would break the flow of the report or distract the reader. If the answer is 'no', place it in the main body of the report, after, and as close as possible to the point of reference. If the answer is 'yes', put it in an appendix.

When **choosing** appropriate illustrations, your aim is to include artwork which arouses readers' interest and helps them to a quicker and fuller understanding. Do not try to be clever. Use clear, simple, uncluttered and appropriate illustrations, concentrating on the essentials.

A picture should save a thousand words; it should not generate another thousand words.

Illustrations have one of three main functions:

- to give a general impression
- to show detailed information
- to show the structure and working of a system.

Use the kinds of illustration that best serve your purpose.

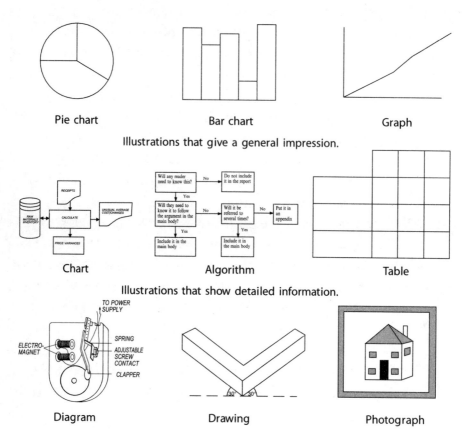

Pie chart   Bar chart   Graph

Illustrations that give a general impression.

Chart   Algorithm   Table

Illustrations that show detailed information.

Diagram   Drawing   Photograph

Illustrations that show the structure and working of a system.

Appropriateness is the key to effectiveness.

Whenever you include illustrations, bear these points in mind:

- Make sure that any artwork is viewed at the same distance as the text – a reader should not have to hold a page closer or farther away when looking at an illustration.

- Refer to illustrations and explain their significance in the text *before* they appear, not after.

- Do not overdo it; too many illustrations will overwhelm the reader. One large simple image is far more eye-catching than half a dozen small ones.

MAKING WHAT MATTERS WORK FOR YOU

✓ **Appearance matters**. Reports of today can be made to look far more attractive and appealing than reports of yesterday. Be sure that your reports look **interesting** and make people **want to read them.**

✓ The key to effective presentation is to consider your readers when deciding the layout of a report. And readers are used to plenty of **white space**. If you are really concerned about the future of the Scandinavian forests, the amount of paper saved by careful preparation and planning will more than compensate for an extra few pages in the report.

✓ A **picture** (or other illustration) can save a thousand words, providing it's the right picture, and in the right place.

Putting it into Practice

1 Make sure you carefully prepare and plan your report

- Set your objective

- Assess your readership

- Decide what information you will need

- Prepare your skeletal framework

2 Gather together the information you need

- Locate the information

- Obtain the information

- Record your findings

- Evaluate and prioritise your findings

- Collate, sort and group your findings

3 Write and revise your report

- Start by pre-writing and taking an overview

- Draft the main body and any appendices

- Draft your conclusions, recommendations, introduction and summary

- Check and amend your report

- Issue your report

4 Write in an appropriate style

- Make sure your report is readable

- Write in a style that suits your readership

- Never be totally satisfied with your writing

5 Make sure you use good English

- Bear in mind basic grammar

- Consider the syntax of your writing

- Check that you have used punctuation correctly

- Choose your words carefully

- Check that your spelling is correct

6 Add the final touches

- Use a word-processing or desktop publishing system to create a polished and readable report

- Refine the layout and design

- Use appropriate illustrations to enhance your report